1989
The Year I Was Born

Compiled by Sally Tagholm

Illustrated by Michael Evans

Puffin Books
in association with Signpost Books

PUFFIN BOOKS

Published by the Penguin Group
Penguin Books Ltd, 27 Wrights Lane, London W8 5TZ, England
Penguin Books USA Inc., 375 Hudson Street, New York, NY 10014, USA
Penguin Books Australia Ltd, Ringwood, Victoria, Australia
Penguin Books Canada Ltd, 10 Alcorn Avenue, Toronto, Ontario, Canada M4V 3B2
Penguin Books (NZ) Ltd, 182–190 Wairau Road, Auckland 10, New Zealand

Penguin Books Ltd, Registered Offices: Harmondsworth, Middlesex, England

Published by Penguin Books in association with Signpost Books

First published 1994
10 9 8 7 6 5 4 3 2 1

Based on an original idea by Sally Wood
Conceived, designed and produced by Signpost Books Ltd, 1994

Editor: Dorothy Wood
Art Director: Treld Bicknell
Paste up: Naomi Games

ISBN 1 874785 10 4 Hardback edition
ISBN 0140 37401 9 Paperback edition

Colour separations by Fotographics, Ltd.
Printed and bound in Belgium by Proost Book Production through Landmark Production Consultants, Ltd.

Typeset by DP Photosetting, Aylesbury, Bucks

MY FAMILY

Name: Abigail
Date of birth: 07.03.89
Time of birth:
Place of birth:
Weight at birth:
Colour of eyes: blue.
Colour of hair (if any): blonde.
Distinguishing marks:

January

Sunday January 1

More than 100 hot-air balloons take off from 98 cities all over France to launch celebrations for the 200th anniversary of the French Revolution.

Monday January 2

Bank Holiday. An oil slick, first reported on Dec 27, slithers along the English Channel to Dorset.

Tuesday January 3

Mark Duncan (19) sets off from his home in Hailsham, East Sussex, at 10am to walk nearly 14,000km round the coast of Britain in aid of Marie Curie Cancer Care.

Wednesday January 4

Birmingham City Council forbids the sale of sweets that contain a red food colouring called amaranth, or E123. It was banned in the US 12 years ago.

Thursday January 5

Snow falls in the Khur desert, Iran, for the first time in 50 years. Hilary, a 13-month-old wire-haired fox terrier, is named 'Pup of the Year' in London.

Friday January 6

Emperor Hirohito of Japan (87), dies at 9.33pm GMT, bringing to an end the era known as Showa or 'Enlightened Peace'. He had reigned for 63 years and was the oldest monarch in the world.

Saturday January 7

The Lord Mayor of London invites more than 500 guests to a Children's Party at the Mansion House. New Moon

Sunday January 8

A new winter steam train service starts today on the Watercress Line between Alresford and Alton, Hants.

Monday January 9

Scientists begin tests at Bristol University on a 40,000 year old piece of mammoth skin from the Soviet Union.

Tuesday January 10

John McCarthy, the British journalist who was kidnapped in the Lebanon, spends his 1,000th day in captivity. His friends hold a vigil outside the Iranian Embassy in London and present a petition to No. 10 Downing Street.

Wednesday January 11

The Great Ormond Street Children's Hospital Wishing Well Appeal reaches £42,000,000. Sir Christopher Collet, Lord Mayor of London, launches a year of celebrations to mark the 800th anniversary of the office of Lord Mayor of London.

Thursday January 12

Watch out for Giant Japanese Knotweed! The Welsh Development Agency declares war on the Oriental plant that grows more than 3m tall and is invading hedgerows and riverbanks.

January

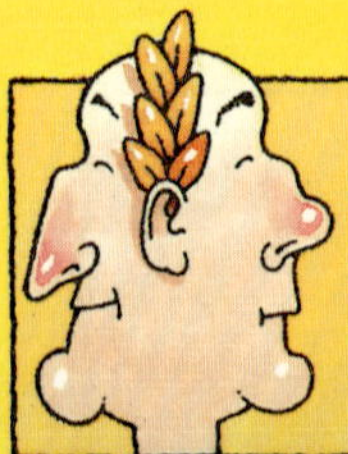

Named after the Roman God, Janus, who had two faces and could look backwards and forwards at the same time; also known as 'frosty month', 'after-yule', 'first-month' and 'snow-month'.

The Lord Mayoralty of London

Sir Christopher Collet, who is the 661st Lord Mayor of London, launches a special year of celebrations to mark the 800th anniversary of the office of Lord Mayor by cutting a giant birthday cake at Guildhall. It is more than 2m tall, almost 1.25m wide at the base and weighs over a tonne! Baked by the National Bakery School, the cake contains 72.5kg sultanas, 72.5kg currants, 59kg brown sugar and 54kg of almond paste. On top of the six-tier cake is a marzipan figure of Dick Whittington, the most famous of all the Lord Mayors of London.

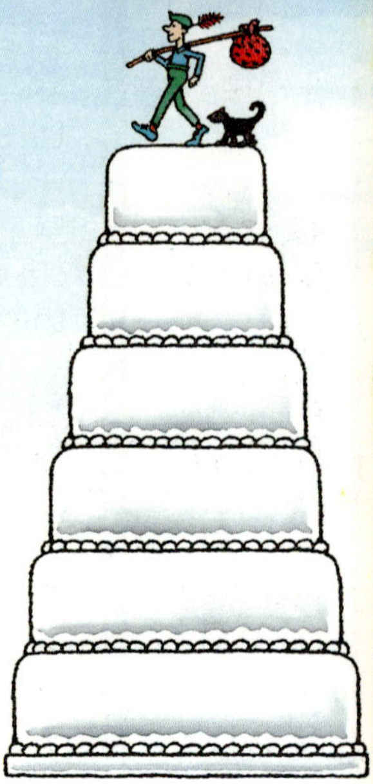

There are many anniversary events throughout the year, including concerts and banquets, a visit by the Lord Mayor's golden coach to the 'Blue Peter' studio and a Dick Whittington Charity Walk from Gloucestershire to London. The Royal Mint issues an 800th Anniversary Medal and the Post Office commemorates the year with a special set of stamps.

Henry Fitz Ailwyn was made the first Lord Mayor of London in 1189—the first year of King Richard I's reign. He stayed in office until he died in 1212.

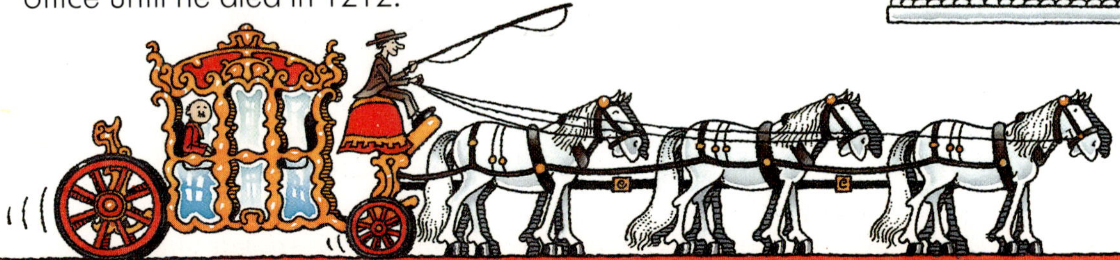

January 16 PO issues 4 new stamps to mark the centenary of the RSPB

Friday January 13

236 silver Roman coins, found in a field on the Membury Farm Estate nr Swindon, Wilts, are declared Treasure Trove, which means that they belong to the Queen.

Gale force winds in Scotland

Saturday January 14

A 270kg bomb from World War II is defused by the Royal Engineers at a quarry near Plymouth. Helicopters rescue 32 people from 42,000 tonne carrier *Yarrawonga*, which is sinking 400km west of Ireland in gale force winds.

Sunday January 15

The Mexican Navy helps to free 31 pilot whales stranded in the Bay of La Paz on the Baja California peninsula.

Monday January 16

In honour of the centenary of the RSPB, the Prime Minister, Mrs Thatcher, names a new BR locomotive 'Avocet', after the black and white wader, which is its symbol, at King's Cross station, London. The European Figure Skating Championships begin at the National Exhibition Centre Arena, Birmingham.

Tuesday January 17

Actor Jeremy Brett, who plays the TV Sherlock Holmes, is chosen as Pipe Smoker of the Year in London. The A50 nr Ashbourne, Derbyshire, is blocked for 1hr after a lorry spills nearly 900 litres of milk.

Wednesday January 18

Calm, mild weather means that the air pollution levels in London from car and lorry fumes are dangerously high.

Thursday January 19

Sir Ranulph Fiennes paddles along the river Thames at Westminster on a floating sledge to test it for his Arctic expedition in March. It will be his third attempt to reach the North Pole without dogs, motor vehicles or aircraft.

Friday January 20

Republican George Bush (64) is sworn in as the 41st President of the United States of America. He takes his oath of office in front of the Capitol in Washington. The north Norfolk coast between Holme and Salthouse becomes a Special Protection Area to preserve endangered birds.

Saturday January 21

A 4000-tonne anti-submarine frigate *Marlborough* is launched from Swan Hunter's Naval yard on the Tyne. It cost £150,000,000.

Full Moon

Sunday January 22

More than 1000 people die in an earthquake which measures 5.3 on the Richter Scale in the Soviet Central Asian Republic of Tajikstan.

Monday January 23

The famous surrealist painter Salvador Dali (84), dies in Figueras, Spain.

Tuesday January 24 — The Duchess of York launches Museums Year 1989 in London to celebrate the 100th birthday of the Museums Association.

Wednesday January 25 — American jazz trumpeter Dizzy Gillespie is made an honorary chieftain and is given the title 'Bashere of Iperu' during a visit to Nigeria.

Thursday January 26 — Australia Day. 18,000,000 listeners in the Soviet Union tune in to hear ex-Beatle Paul McCartney take part in a live phone-in radio programme broadcast from London.

Friday January 27 — It is so warm for the time of year that birds are practising the Dawn Chorus and some blackbirds have begun laying eggs! Sir Thomas Sopwith (101), one of the great pioneers of British aviation, dies.

Saturday January 28 — A record 100 competitors take part in the Spillers Siberian Husky Club Snow Rally at Glenmore Forest, nr Aviemore, Scotland. The Jorvik Viking Festival in York starts with a spectacular firework display at Clifford's Tower.

Sunday January 29 — Thousands of children take part in an RSPB Common Bird Survey to find the ten most common birds in gardens and parks. The Soviet spacecraft *Phobos*, which was launched last year, goes into orbit round Mars.

Monday January 30 — A rare Scandinavian arctic redpole finch settles down in woods near Thorpe End, Norwich. Egyptian archaeologists discover 5 life-sized granite statues from 1470 BC nr the Temple of Luxor in Egypt.

Tuesday January 31 — The Royal Mint holds a special ceremony in the Tower of London to commemorate the 500th anniversary of the Gold Sovereign.

*Top Ten Videos**

1 A Fish Called Wanda
2 Fatal Attraction
3 Good Morning Vietnam
4 Coming to America
5 Buster
6 Crocodile Dundee 2
7 Twins
8 Who Framed Roger Rabbit?
9 Rainman
10 Beetlejuice

* compiled by MRIB

*Top Ten Toys**

1 Transformers (Hasbro)
2 Model kits (various)
3 Masters of the Universe (Mattel)
4 Pre-school toys (Fisher Price)
5 My Little Pony (Hasbro)
6 Timball/Loloball
7 Lego Town (Lego)
8 Care Bears (Kenner Parker)
9 Duplo (Lego)
10 Tomytime (Tomy)

* National Association of Toy Retailers

February

Wednesday February 1
A 16km oil slick is reported in the Antarctic after an Argentine oceanograph ship, *Bahia Paraiso*, sinks in the Bismark Strait.

Thursday February 2
About 300 twitchers flock to see a rare double-crested cormorant from North America on Charlton's Pond at Billingham, Cleveland.

Friday February 3
Thousands of people are evacuated from their homes in the East End of London as army experts steam explosives out of a 454kg World War II bomb, found on a building site in Whitechapel.

Saturday February 4
The annual 'Pot a Pigeon' campaign is held in East Anglia: farmers get their own back on thousands of birds who ruin valuable crops.

Sunday February 5
Sky Channel, Britain's first satellite television station, starts broadcasting at 6pm. The annual Clowns' Service is held at Holy Trinity Church, Dalston, E. London, in memory of Joseph Grimaldi, the famous clown who died in 1837.

Monday February 6
Beginning of the Chinese Year of the Snake. Accession Day, the anniversary of the Queen's accession to the throne, is marked by gun salutes in Hyde Park and at the Tower of London.

New Moon

Tuesday February 7
Pancake Day. Live sardines rain down during a storm in Ipswich, Australia, nearly 50km inland from Brisbane, on the coast. 200 Gordon Highlanders and 70,000 sandbags save Inverness from flooding, after the river Ness bursts its banks.

Wednesday February 8
First day of Lent. The East Surrey Water Company applies for a drought order after the dry, sunny winter.

Thursday February 9
The first American golden-winged warbler ever seen in Britain is spotted in Lunsford Park, Larkfield, nr Maidstone, Kent.

Friday February 10
Tony Robinson, who was born in Jamaica, is elected the first black Sheriff of Nottingham. Astronomers in Chile watch the birth of a pulsar which rotates 2000 times each second because its gravity is so strong. It is a remnant from the inner core of a star.

Saturday February 11
The first snow this season falls at Aviemore in the Cairngorms. Barrington Williams breaks the 23-year-old British indoor long jump record with a leap of 8.05 metres.

Sunday February 12
Champion Potterdale Classic of Moonhill (Cassie for short), a grey-and-white bearded collie bitch, from Botley, nr Southampton, wins the Best in Show title at Crufts, London.

Monday February 13	Hurricane force winds sweep Scotland, the north of England and Northern Ireland—with a record gust of 225kph at Fraserburgh, Grampian. A 6.35cm iron meteor crashes through the roof of the railway station at Lewes, Sussex.
Tuesday February 14	Gales devastate the country: the tide fails to turn in the Thames Estuary because of water driven along the East Coast by storms.
Wednesday February 15	A 5000 tonne Swedish cargo ship, the *Tor Gothia*, which ran aground on the Haisborough Sands, 16kms off the Norfolk coast, is refloated and freed by a tug.
Thursday February 16	A blue-eyed doll, made in Germany in 1909, is sold for £90,200 at Sotheby's, London.

February

The Roman month of purification. It has also been known as 'sprout kale', 'rain-month', 'month of cakes' and 'month of ravaging wolves'.

Happy 100th Birthday to the Royal Society for the Protection of Birds!

The first meeting of what became the RSPB was held in February 1889 at the home of Mrs Robert Williamson in Didsbury, Manchester. She arranged the meeting for people who, like her, were horrified by the latest fashion for feathers. Thousands of egrets, birds of paradise, kingfishers, swallows and owls were killed every year so that their feathers could be used for boas or to adorn the smartest hats. All members of the new Society had to sign a pledge not to wear feathers. Their first campaign against the plumage trade was supported by famous people like the Duchess of Portland and the Ranee of Sarawak. In 1904 the Society was granted a Royal Charter and in 1928 it acquired its first reserve at Romney Marsh, Kent.

RSPB 1989

President: Magnus Magnusson
Symbol: Avocet
Headquarters: Sandy, Beds.
Adult members: 440,000
Junior members: 107,000
Bird reserves: 114

UK Ten Most Common Birds

1 Starling
2 House Sparrow
3 Blue Tit
4 Blackbird
5 Gulls
6 Chaffinch
7 Robin
8 Greenfinch
9 Great Tit
10 Crow

Friday February 17

The RSPB celebrates its 100th birthday at its original home in Didsbury, Manchester, where a special 1989 Time Capsule is buried in the garden and children from Beaver Road School sing 'Happy Birthday' before releasing 100 balloons.

Saturday February 18

Fumio Niwa, a Japanese balloonist trying to cross the Pacific Ocean, is picked up by a fishing boat about 2170km south east of Tokyo.

Sunday February 19

Happy 50th Birthday, Batman! He first appeared in a comic strip cartoon by Bob Kane on February 19, 1939, in *Detective Comics*, published by National Publications.

Full Moon

Monday February 20

The Louvre, the biggest museum in France, shuts for spring cleaning until the end of March. It's the longest the building has been closed since it opened 186 years ago.

Tuesday February 21

The Soviet Union *Phobos 2* spacecraft orbits Mars at 6400km and sends back the first nine pictures of its moon, Phobos.

Wednesday February 22

Watch out if you're driving along the A165 in North Yorkshire! Badgers have dug their homes under a stretch of the road near Filey and about 30 metres of the surface has subsided.

Thursday February 23

The Prime Minister, Mrs Thatcher, promises that pints of milk, beer and cider, as well as miles on road signs, will not go metric.

Friday February 24

The body of Emperor Hirohito of Japan, who died on January 6, is entombed in a £12,000,000 mausoleum after a 13hr funeral ceremony in Shinjuku Gardens, Tokyo.

Heavy snow in North

Saturday February 25

Snow causes havoc in the North with about 300 motorists stranded in the Peak District. Over 15cms of snow falls on Exmoor. Boxing champion Mike Tyson (USA) defeats Frank Bruno (GB) in the World Heavyweight title fight in Las Vegas, USA.

Sunday February 26

Ennerdale and Kinniside village school, nr Cleator in West Cumbria, is awarded a gold star by Her Majesty's Inspectors.

Monday February 27

A baby gorilla called Kibam is born at Howlett's Zoo Park near Canterbury, Kent. She weighs 1.5kg.

Tuesday February 28

A plaque to the poet Matthew Arnold (1822–88) is unveiled in Poets' Corner, Westminster Abbey, London.

UK Fact File 1989

British Food and Farming Year

Museums Year

Europe Against Cancer Year

Total area of the United Kingdom	244,100sq kms
Capital City	London (1580sq kms)
Population of UK	57,236,000

Births
777,300

Deaths 657,700

Marriages
392,042

Divorces
164,916

Most popular girl's name*

Most popular boy's name*

Head of State Queen Elizabeth II

Prime Minister
Margaret Hilda Thatcher

Poet Laureate
Edward (Ted) Hughes

Astronomer Royal
Prof. Sir Francis Graham Smith

Royal Swan Keeper
F.J. Turk

Archbishop of Canterbury
Robert Alexander Kennedy Runcie

Members of Parliament: 650 (523 for England, 38 for Wales, 72 for Scotland and 17 for N. Ireland). 41 are women

Presidency of EEC

Spain (Jan–June)

France (July–Dec)

Members of EEC: Belgium, Denmark, France, Federal Republic of Germany, Greece, Ireland, Italy, Luxembourg, The Netherlands, Portugal, Spain, the United Kingdom

* according to *The Times* newspaper

March

Wednesday
March 1

St David's Day: dragon-shaped loaves called Dewi (David) are sold in Newport, Gwent. Watch out for B9 – a gigantic 150km × 35km iceberg which broke off the Ross Ice Shelf last year and is slowly melting in Antarctic waters!

Thursday
March 2

Thousands of 4cm surgical needles fall off the back of a vehicle travelling along the M6 causing multiple punctures near Walsall.

Friday
March 3

Happy 104th birthday to Mrs Myfanwy Evans of Colwyn Bay, Clwyd. A new junior version of the Highway Code is launched.

Saturday
March 4

The first Snail Seminar is held at the Royal Museum, Edinburgh, to encourage indoor snail farming in the UK. The Giant African Snail (Achatina) is particularly recommended because it grows very quickly. Snail pate, snail vol-au-vents, and snails on sticks are served.

Sunday
March 5

Mothering Sunday. The QE2 is battered by gale force winds and 12m waves in the Pacific Ocean on her way from Los Angeles to Auckland. 41 people are treated for cuts and bruises.

Monday
March 6

The European Space Agency's *Ariane 4* rocket is launched from Guyana. A huge solar flare spouts on the surface of the sun: it's one of the strongest ever recorded!

17°C in London

Tuesday
March 7

Beer goes on sale in Iceland this month for the first time since it was banned at the beginning of the century. A partial eclipse of the Sun is visible from parts of the Pacific, North America and Greenland.

New Moon

Wednesday
March 8

No Smoking Day. International Women's Day. The Queen travels 6746.6km in 4hrs 8mins, flying by Concorde from Heathrow Airport, London, to Barbados in the West Indies.

Thursday
March 9

According to the annual Pocket Money Monitor, which is published today, average pocket money has risen by 14% over the last year to £1.40 per week.

Friday
March 10

Comic Relief Day II: 50,000 events take place all over the country. These include policemen in Leytonstone directing the traffic dressed as garden gnomes, a giant Cheddar cheese being pushed from Bristol to Cheddar Gorge and the Town Hall at Brighton being wrapped in red tape.

Saturday
March 11

100 British holidaymakers are stuck at Luxor in the Egyptian desert when Concorde fails to take off because of flat batteries.

March

Named after Mars, the Roman God of War. It has also been known as 'rough-month', 'lengthening-month', 'boisterous-month' and 'windy-month'.

March 7 PO issues 4 new stamps to celebrate Food and Farming Year

THE T.B.M.

Altogether 11 gigantic Tunnel Boring Machines will crawl slowly under the seabed between Shakespeare Cliff, Dover, and Sangatte, Calais, before the Channel Tunnel is open for business in the mid-1990s. Each monster weighs about 1500 tonnes and is as long as two football pitches. The huge rotating face at the front of the machine is studded with sharp metal teeth that can gouge out the chalk marl under the seabed at 2m an hour.

Over the past two centuries there have been almost 70 different Channel Tunnel schemes. The first, in 1802, included special ventilation chimneys to the surface of the sea and an island for resting horses on the Varne Sandbank in the middle of the Channel. Nearly 80 years later, an Englishman called Colonel Beaumont tunnelled almost 2000m from both sides until he was stopped because politicians were worried about the danger of invasion.

Great Balls of Fire!

The sun is at the peak of its 11-year cycle in 1989 with a record number of sunspots (solar storms) on its surface. March is a particularly eventful month with the largest solar flare ever recorded by the Solar Maximum Mission satellite, which has been in orbit since 1980. This is followed by ten more extremely strong flares during the next fortnight, as well as 60 smaller ones. These cause huge geomagnetic storms which interfere with orbiting satellites, affect electricity grids on Earth and make it hard for racing pigeons to navigate. They are also responsible for the most dazzling display of the Aurora Borealis or Northern Lights for 50yrs. The bright coloured lights, which are usually seen only in the north, fill the night sky all over the country.

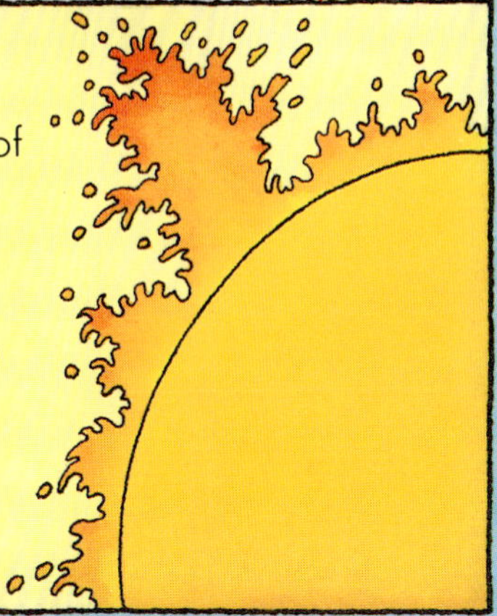

Sunday March 12

25 crewmen are rescued by 6 helicopters and 2 lifeboats off the coast of Cornwall when their 2,667 tonne cargo ship *Secil Japan* is driven onto the rocks at Hell's Mouth nr Padstow in force 11 gales.

Monday March 13

Commonwealth Day. US space shuttle *Discovery* is launched from Cape Canaveral, Florida, on a 5-day mission—with a 5-man crew, 4 rats, 32 fertilized hens' eggs and a small garden of lilies and weeds.

Tuesday March 14

Budget Day. Sir Ranulph Fiennes and Dr Mike Stroud set off from Ward Hunt Island, N. Canada, in temperatures of –58°C to walk unaided the 684km to the North Pole.

Wednesday March 15

The Prince and Princess of Wales watch a camel race in the desert at Al-Ain in the United Arab Emirates during their Gulf Tour.

Thursday March 16

Sir Ranulph Fiennes and Dr Mike Stroud abandon their trek to the North Pole after only 2 days because of heavy snowfalls and melting pack ice. *Desert Orchid* (5–2 favourite) becomes the first grey to win the Gold Cup at Cheltenham.

Friday March 17

St Patrick's Day. The Transport Minister, Paul Channon, starts up the £8,000,000 Tunnel Boring Machine (TBM) at the official launch of the Channel train tunnel from Shakespeare's Cliff, near Dover, Kent.

Saturday March 18

The US space shuttle *Discovery* lands safely at Edward Air Force Base in the Californian desert after a successful 5-day mission.

Sunday March 19

27th annual Concours International du Meilleur Boudin, or International Black Pudding Championships, are held at Mortagne-au-Perche, Normandy, France.

Monday March 20

The Spring Equinox, when the sun crosses the equator from south to north, occurs at 3.28pm. British explorer Robert Swan and an international Icewalk team set out from Cape Aldrich, N. Canada, on a 756km trek to the North Pole in temperatures of –55°C.

Gale force winds bring snow and heavy rain across the country

Tuesday March 21

Happy 75th Birthday to the Brownies! A special party is held at their headquarters in Buckingham Palace Road, London. A Roman lead coffin, found in a garden in St Albans, Herts, is opened at the Verulamium Museum to reveal the skeleton of a 1.8m man who died in the 3rd or 4th century.

Wednesday March 22	The Hindu spring festival of Holi. The only known example of a George III penny is sold for £9,460 at auction in London. Earth has a close encounter of 690,000km with a small asteroid that hurtles past tonight at 74,000kph.   Full Moon
Thursday March 23	Maundy Thursday: the Queen presents Maundy money to 63 men and 63 women at Birmingham Cathedral in a special ceremony that dates back to the 12th century.
Friday March 24	Good Friday. Paddy Graham, of London, wins the British Marbles Championship at Tinsley Green, W. Sussex. The Black Dog Boozers win the team event. A chick hatches at Louisville, Kentucky, from one of the 32 hens' eggs that orbited Earth for 5 days on board US space shuttle *Discovery*. 
Saturday March 25	Oxford wins 135th University Boat Race, beating Cambridge by 2½ lengths in 18mins 27secs. For the first time ever, both crews are coxed by women. 
Sunday March 26	Easter Sunday. British Summer Time starts at 1am when clocks go forward by one hour. England's only pair of breeding Golden Eagles lay their first egg of the year near Haweswater in the Lake District.
Monday March 27	Bank Holiday. Mark Ryder (27) eats a pound of fried baby eels in 35secs and wins the world elver-eating championship for the 6th year running. 26th World Coal Carrying Championships are held at Gaythorpe, Ossett, West Yorks. 
Tuesday March 28	The Governor of Alaska declares Prince William Sound and the port of Valdez a disaster area after the supertanker *Exxon Valdez* runs aground, spilling over 45,460,000 litres of crude oil.
Wednesday March 29	President Mitterand of France inaugurates a spectacular new glass pyramid in the Cour Napoleon at the Louvre, Paris. It has to be cleaned once a month by special window cleaners who are qualified climbers and known as *'laveurs alpinistes'*. 
Thursday March 30	Robert Swan and the international team of explorers, who set off from northern Canada 10 days ago, have now trekked 64km towards the North Pole in soft thick snow and temperatures of –42°C. 20°C in London—the hottest March day in the capital for 21 years
Friday March 31	The Eiffel Tower in Paris celebrates its 100th birthday. Richard Branson hovers over the M25 in Surrey in a silver balloon with flashing lights pretending to be a UFO.

April

Saturday
April 1

County councils all over the country celebrate their centenary. In Berkshire councillors wear 19th century dress at Shire Hall, Reading, to re-enact the council's first meeting in 1889.

Sunday
April 2

A fleet of 5 helicopters start scooping up 8,000,000 fledgeling salmon from freshwater Scottish lochs and flying them to new sea water homes on the west coast. 'Young Magician of the Year' finals are held at the Polka Children's Theatre in Wimbledon.

Monday
April 3

The cricket bat industry is threatened by an epidemic of watermark disease which is spreading from the white bat willow (salix alba) to the weeping willow (salix babylonica).

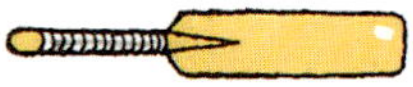

Tuesday
April 4

Happy 40th birthday to NATO! An African cycad, which was brought to the Royal Botanic Gardens, Kew, in 1775, is rehoused in the newly restored Palm House.

Wednesday
April 5

More than 12cms of snow falls over the south of England with Surrey, Berkshire, Oxfordshire and Buckinghamshire worst affected. David Gower is chosen as captain of the English cricket team.

Thursday
April 6

Scientists claim to have discovered the worst smell in the world. It is revolting, disgusting and vile, and so nasty that simply smearing it on the trunks of maple trees turns the syrup sour.

New Moon

Friday
April 7

First day of Ramadan. National No Smoking Day in France. The Soviet President, Mikhail Gorbachev, has lunch with the Queen at Windsor Castle.

Saturday
April 8

5th International Clown Convention starts at Bognor Regis, Sussex. 12-yr-old *Polveir* (28–1), ridden by Jimmy Frost, wins the Grand National at Aintree by 7 lengths. The prize is £66,840.

Sunday
April 9

The British catamaran *Chaffoteaux Challenger*, which left New York yesterday in a bid to break the Transatlantic speed record, is blown off course by strong northerly winds.

Monday
April 10

The Young Citizens Awards are presented in a ceremony at the Mansion House, London. The Princess Royal opens a new £40,000,000 shopping centre at Clayton Square, Liverpool.

Tuesday
April 11

Gales sweep across Britain with a 159kph gust recorded in Milford Haven, Dyfed. A railway building is blown down in Birmingham, and two airliners are blown off the ground at Manchester airport.

April

The opening month—from the Latin 'aperire', which means to open. Also known as the time of budding, the cuckoo's May or the fool's May.

Icewalk to the North Pole

Team

Robert Swan (UK)
Rupert Summerson (UK)
Graeme Day (Australia)
Misha Malakhov (USSR)
Arved Fuchs (W. Germany)
Hiroshin Onishi (Japan)
Angus Cockney (Canada)
Darryl Roberts (USA)

Robert Swan and his team take 55 days to reach the North Pole after setting out from Cape Aldrich in the far north of Canada on March 20. Each man is equipped with skis and pulls a 68kg sledge. They clamber over huge 12m ice scrapers and ski across vast tracts of frozen ice floes, covering between 4.8km and 24km each day. With temperatures as low as -55°C, their sweat freezes under layers of clothes and frostbite attacks feet, fingers and faces. After a long day's trek they pitch their tents and tuck into a diet of pemmican, butter, oil, powdered milk and reconstituted foods. Beneath their sleeping bags, the frozen Arctic Ocean creaks and groans. Towards the end of April the weather warms unusually quickly to -15°C and the pack ice starts to break up, revealing dangerous long black 'leads' of water below. It is now a race against the Arctic spring and the team begins travelling at night when the temperature is lower and the water frozen. After 756km they reach the North Pole on May 14. Robert Swan, who reached the South Pole in 1986, becomes the first person ever to have walked to both ends of the world. His mascot is also, quite probably, the first teddy bear in history to visit both North and South Poles.

April 11 PO issues 4 new Anniversaries stamps

Wednesday April 12

Donald Ritchie, from Lossiemouth, Grampian, sets a new record for the 1327km John O'Groats to Land's End run of 10 days 15hrs 27mins. 8 Swedish frogs, due to be sent into space to mate, escape before the rocket is launched.

Thursday April 13

'Dinosaurs Live' exhibition opens at the Natural History Museum, London, complete with life-sized computer-controlled prehistoric monsters.

Friday April 14

Greater Flamingos have started to lay their eggs at the Wildfowl and Wetlands Trust, Slimbridge, Gloucs, today—much earlier than usual.

Saturday April 15

Start of the cricket season. Robert Swan and the Icewalk team, who left for the North Pole on March 20, have lost radio contact with base camp and 5 of the team have frostbite.

Sunday April 16

Hugh Edeleanu drives 1465km from John O'Groats to Land's End in a custom-built, turbo-charged JCB digger in 35hrs and sets a new world record.

Monday April 17

The British catamaran *Chaffoteaux Challenger* is rescued by a container ship 885km off the Azores after storms force the crew to abandon their attempt on the Transatlantic speed record.

Tuesday April 18

A hot-air balloon crash-lands on the main road in Chelmsford, Essex. Luxembourg celebrates the 150th anniversary of independence from Belgian rule.

Wednesday April 19

Actors and actresses take part in Shakespeare's 425th Birthday Marathon Reading at the Theatre Museum, Covent Garden, London. They read extracts from his complete works every day until his birthday on Sunday.

Thursday April 20

First day of Passover. One-day Tube strike in London. A Royal Navy bomb disposal team carries out a controlled explosion off Margate, Kent, after a fishing trawler nets a 680kg wartime German mine.

Friday April 21

Happy 63rd Birthday to the Queen! The Royal Horse Artillery fires the 41-gun salute from Green Park because Hyde Park is busy preparing for the Festival of Food and Farming in May

Full Moon

Saturday April 22

A hot-air balloon called *Rainbow Endeavour* flies over the North Pole carrying the message SAVE THE OZONE LAYER. It floats at 305m and collects samples of Arctic air.

Sunday April 23

22,406 runners finish the London Marathon: Veronique Marot (France) is the fastest woman in 2hrs 25mins 26secs and Douglas Wakiihuri (Kenya) is the fastest man in 2hrs 9mins 3secs.

Monday April 24

Matthew Rollston (8), from Co. Down, N. Ireland, is chosen as Superkid of the Year in London. Severely disabled after an accident, he has learned to swim, climb and play football.

It's -8°C in Eskdalemuir, Dumfries & Galloway tonight

Tuesday April 25

A 1648 gold coin is sold for £29,150 at Christie's, London. On one face it has the name of Charles II and on the other it has the motto of Charles I '*Dum Spiro Spero*' (While I breathe I hope).

Wednesday April 26

Supplies of chocolate, bacon, pepper salami, batteries and fuel—as well as a new sleeping bag—are delivered by a Twin Otter support plane to the Icewalk team.

Thursday April 27

Three Soviet cosmonauts touch down in Kazakhstan, Central Asia, from the orbiting space station *Mir*, leaving it empty for the first time in 2yrs.

Friday April 28

More than 1000 people arrive at White Horse Hill, Uffington, Oxon, to celebrate the ancient festival of Beltane on Dragon Hill.

Saturday April 29

There are celebrations in New York this weekend to mark the 200th anniversary of George Washington's inauguration as the first President of the United States.

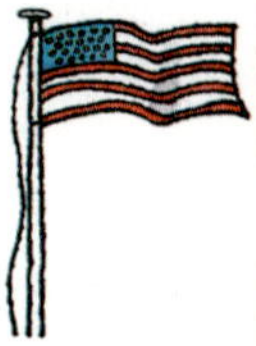

Sunday April 30

Beginning of the first National Pet Week. Steve Brace, from Britain, wins the Paris Marathon in 2hrs 13mins 3secs.

The British Family 1989

Mr and Mrs 1989 and the little 1989s each drink, on average, 2.23 litres of milk and cream each week. They eat 115.38g of cheese, 1.02kg of meat, 147g of fish, 2.29 eggs, 268.75g of fat and oil, 233g of sugar and preserves, 3.24kg of fresh fruit and vegetables, 1.5kg bread and cereals and drink 73.71g of beverages.

On average, they watch television for 25½ hours a week and send 46 Christmas cards to family and friends.

(These figures are taken from the National Food Survey.)

May

Monday
May 1

Bank Holiday. Tower of London ravens, Charlie and Rhys, become parents. Their chick, Ronnie, is the first raven to be born at the Tower for 300 years!

Tuesday
May 2

The Prince of Wales talks to Jimmy Young on Radio 2 at 11am. Miss Betty Boothroyd, MP for West Bromwich West, wears navy silk robes designed by Hardy Amies, when she takes her place as the first woman deputy speaker of the House of Commons.

Wednesday
May 3

Oxford University Boat Club elects Alison Norrish as its first woman president after she coxed the team to victory in this year's Boat Race.

Thursday
May 4

Mrs Thatcher celebrates her 10th anniversary as Prime Minister. US space shuttle *Atlantis* blasts off from Cape Canaveral, Florida, carrying the Magellan space probe at the start of its 450-day journey to Venus.

New Moon 

Friday
May 5

The Festival of Food and Farming opens in Hyde Park, London: with more than 1000 livestock and 350 different stands, it's the biggest show in the park since the Great Exhibition of 1851.

Saturday
May 6

Water-skiing champion, Steve Butterworth (32) from Halifax, who has only one leg, becomes the first person to ski across the Irish Sea. It takes him 4hrs, 51mins and 42secs to cross the 113km from Holyhead, Anglesea, to Howth, nr Dublin.

Sunday
May 7

Mr Punch celebrates his 327th birthday at a special service in St Paul's Church, Covent Garden, London. Afterwards a street party is held with stilt walkers, strong men and clowns.

Monday
May 8

World Red Cross Day. The Museum of the River is opened by the Prince of Wales at the Ironbridge Gorge Museum, Telford, Salop.

Tuesday
May 9

18 earth tremors shake the Canary Islands today: the strongest measures 4.5 on the Richter Scale. A Picasso self-portrait is sold for £27,000,000 in New York.

Wednesday
May 10

President Bush announces that the new US space shuttle will be called *Endeavour*, after the 18th century British ship which Capt. Cook sailed to Tahiti to record the transit of Venus in 1769.

Thursday
May 11

Andrew Lloyd Webber's musical *Cats* celebrates its 8th birthday and becomes the longest-running musical in the West End. It has its 3358th performance tomorrow!

May

Takes its name from Maia, the goddess of growth and increase, or from 'maiores', the Latin word for elders, who were honoured this month. The Anglo Saxons called it 'thrimilce' because cows could be milked three times a day now. An old Dutch name was 'bloumaand' which means blossoming month.

May Feature

The Tower of London is an ancient fortress that dates back to the time of William the Conqueror.

It was a royal residence for centuries and has also housed the Royal Mint and the Royal Menagerie.

It is still the home of six very important large black birds.

According to legend, the Tower and the Crown will fail if the Ravens leave.

So, the birds are looked after very carefully by the Yeoman Ravenmaster

And he keeps two extra Ravens in reserve – just in case.

The birds are called Larry, Cedric, Hugine, Gwylum, Hardey, Charlie, Rhys, and Ronnie.

The Yeoman Ravenmaster feeds them on heart and liver, which he buys from Smithfield market. He sprinkles a good vitamin and mineral supplement on top.

The Ravens also enjoy scraps from the Troops' Kitchen. They are extremely fond of fried bread and the odd par-boiled egg.

During the day the birds flap around the White Tower. Sometimes they bury their food in the ground to hide it from unwelcome visitors.

To make sure that they don't flap too far the Yeoman Ravenmaster and his wife trim their wings every few weeks.

At night the Raven's sleep in cages that look like left-luggage lockers.

Charlie and Rhys build their nest in a special wooden breeding house that could be mistaken for a medieval beach hut.

When their precious egg hatches, the chick is named after ex president Ronald Reagan who visits London this year.

Friday
May 12

21m power boat *Ilan Voyager* arrives back in Brighton after setting a new non-stop round-Britain record of 72hrs 54mins (clockwise).

Saturday
May 13

400 teams take part in the 30th Ten Tors expedition across Dartmoor. 40 Canberras, Britain's first jet bombers, give a flying display at RAF Wyton, Cambs, to celebrate their 40th birthday.

Sunday
May 14

National Windmill Day. Robert Swan becomes the first person to walk to both ends of the Earth when he and his Icewalk team reach the North Pole after a 55 day 756km trek.

Monday
May 15

Hundreds of Scottish fishermen flock to Loch Aline, north of Oban, Argyllshire, after 7000 juicy 3.5kg salmon escape from a fish farm. The government agrees to delay building work on the site of the Elizabethan Rose Theatre, Southwark, after an all-night vigil by actors and archaeologists.

Tuesday
May 16

The Home Office lowers the height minimum for the Fire Brigade by 2.5cms to 1.54m in a bid to recruit more females into the service.

Wednesday
May 17

Roads Minister Peter Bottomley says that the average speed of traffic in central London is now 17.7kph. In Rome it's 20.1kph and in Paris it's just under 14.5kph!

Thursday
May 18

An unusual ginger teddy bear, made by Steiff of Germany between 1906 and 1909 for Princess Xenia, a cousin of Tsar Nicholas II, is sold for £12,100 at Christie's, London.

Friday
May 19

The 1000th avocet chick hatches at the RSPB nature reserve at Minsmere, Suffolk. Launch of National Wildflower Week.

Saturday
May 20

Liverpool beats Everton 3–2 in the FA Cup Final and Celtic beats Rangers 1–0 in the Scottish Cup Final.

Full Moon

Sunday
May 21

Hundreds of people set off on a 16-day, 225km charity walk from Pauntley, Gloucs, to retrace Dick Whittington's legendary journey to London. They are celebrating the 800th anniversary of the Lord Mayoralty of London.

28.6°C in Bournemouth and Southampton

Monday
May 22

Beginning of the first National Sleep Out Week. A pedal car auction is held at Sotheby's in Billingshurst, Sussex: a 1905 Belgian Veteran Car fetches £3,740 and a 1929 French Eureka Bugatti is sold for £1,870.

Tuesday May 23

Heatwave continues in the south with temperatures of 27°C. More than 100 people collapse with heat exhaustion, dehydration or blisters at the 76th Chelsea Flower Show in London.

Wednesday May 24

The Queen visits the Channel Islands and opens the first medical centre on Sark (pop. 560).

30°C in London. Thunderstorms and rain over the rest of the country. 5.4cm of rain falls in Farnborough, Surrey

Thursday May 25

Standpipes and tankers are at the ready in London as water supplies are cut because of the heatwave. Emergency bottled water is delivered to the Brompton Hospital, Chelsea.

Friday May 26

The 10,000th edition of 'The Archers' is broadcast on Radio 4. It's 5mins longer than usual so that all the members of the cast can take part.

Saturday May 27

The new £2,000,000 Robin Hood Centre is opened in Nottingham. About 250,000 people in 9 European countries get out their binoculars in a mass Spring Bank Holiday birdwatch.

Sunday May 28

Six members of Lea Manor High School and Community College, Luton, Beds, set a new record when they arrive at the Arc de Triomphe, Paris, after travelling 400.7km from Marble Arch, London, in a pedal car.

Monday May 29

Bank Holiday. 101 cyclists from 12 countries set off from Westminster Bridge, London, at the start of the 1,770km round-Britain Milk Cycle Race, which will finish in Birmingham on June 10.

Tuesday May 30

'Elefriends' is launched at the National Geographical Society, London, to save the African elephant and to ban the sale of ivory all over the world.

Wednesday May 31

Lava erupts from the volcano Kilauea in Hawaii for the first time in a year.

May 16
PO issues 4 new Europe, Toys and Games stamps

June

Thursday June 1	The Asthma Research Council's official pollen count starts today. Wheel clamp release charge in London goes up from £25 to £30.
Friday June 2	The Queen celebrates the 36th anniversary of her coronation. One of Britain's rarest beetles, *Omophlus rufitarsis,* which hasn't been seen for 60yrs, is spotted on a thrift plant on Chesil Beach, Dorset. 
Saturday June 3	Ayatollah Khomeini (86), leader of the Islamic fundamentalist revolution, dies in Tehran.  New Moon
Sunday June 4	France bans all ivory imports. British rock group, Pink Floyd, stages a spectacular £2,000,000 show in Moscow's Olympic stadium.
Monday June 5	World Environment Day. 22 British beaches win the European Blue Flag Award for clean water and litter-free sands. Dick Whittington Charity Walk, which left Pauntley, Gloucs, on May 21, reaches Guildhall, London. 
Tuesday June 6	Snow covers part of Kent with more than 10cms falling in Gillingham. The Queen Mother unveils a new stained-glass window at Bayeux Cathedral, Normandy, on the 45th anniversary of the D-Day landings at the end of World War II.
Wednesday June 7	A collection of medals, awarded to the first cross-Channel swimmer, Captain Matthew Webb, is sold in London for £12,650. It took him almost 22hrs to cross from Admiralty Pier, Dover, to Calais in 1875. 
Thursday June 8	The Duke of Kent takes the salute and pensioners give three cheers for King Charles II on Founder's Day at the Royal Hospital, Chelsea.
Friday June 9	The British freefall parachute record is broken over Peterborough, Cambs, when 60 skydivers join hands at 4572m. 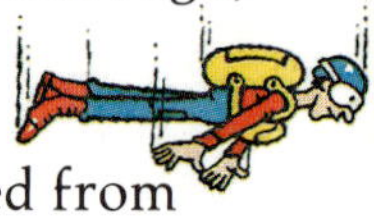
Saturday June 10	Goodbye to Britain's last manned lightship as she is towed from the English Channel into the port of Harwich. The 1770km Milk Cycle Race is won by Brian Walton (Canada).
Sunday June 11	Mary-Elizabeth Raw, from Weston-Super-Mare, wins the BBC's Mastermind title with a score of 33 points. Her specialist subject is the life and reign of Charles I.
Monday June 12	MPs vote 293–69 in favour of televising the House of Commons, starting in November. The Department of Health advises people not to eat hazelnut yogurt after an outbreak of botulism in NW England.

June

Takes its name from Juno, the great Roman goddess of the Moon, or from 'Juniores', the Latin word for young people, who were honoured this month. 'Zomer-maand' in Old Dutch (Summer month) and 'Sere-monath' in Old Saxon (Dry month).

Dick Whittington Charity Walk

According to the well-known story, Dick Whittington left his home in Pauntley, Gloucestershire, and set off to seek his fortune in London. He had heard that the streets were paved with gold, and he wanted to see for himself! As you probably know, he became a very rich man and was elected Lord Mayor three times—in 1397, 1406 and 1419.

This year, as part of the Lord Mayor of London's 800th anniversary celebrations, a special Dick Whittington Walk retraces the famous journey from Gloucestershire to London. Complete with cat, it sets off from Pauntley on May 21 and, averaging 14 miles a day, arrives at Guildhall, London, on June 5.

The route: Pauntley, Gloucester, Cirencester, Lechlade, Bablock Hythe, Oxford, Abingdon, Wallingford, Henley-on-Thames, Maidenhead, Windsor, Weybridge, Richmond, Putney, Highgate, Guildhall.

British Blue Flag Beaches

West Beach, Clacton	Weymouth Central
South Beach, Lowestoft	Cullercoats
Bexhill	Corbyn (Torre Abbey)
Eastbourne	Anstey's Cove/Redgate
Lee-on-Solent	Oddicombe
Poole Shore Road	Quaywest
Bournemouth Pier	Exmouth
Swanage	Sidmouth
Seaton	Blackpool Sands (Devon)
Crinnis	Porthmeor
Sennen Cove	Jacob's Ladder (Sidmouth)

Tuesday June 13

Councillors in Chichester, Sussex, scratch their heads over plans to re-open a disused railway tunnel between Chichester and Sussex where rare mouse-eared bats hibernate.

17°C in London

Wednesday June 14

Two koalas, Billi (7) and Mije (5), arrive at London Zoo from San Diego, California, with a large bunch of eucalyptus leaves. Fresh supplies will be flown across the Atlantic twice a week to keep them happy.

Thursday June 15

A meteorite crashes to Earth near the Bay of Plenty on North Island, New Zealand. The £30,000,000 Portland Vase, believed to have been made for the Roman Emperor Augustus 2000 years ago, goes back on display at the British Museum after being restored.

Friday June 16

The Prince of Wales visits Dorchester, Dorset, to inspect plans for new model villages to be built on Duchy of Cornwall land nr Poundbury Farm.

Saturday June 17

The Queen's Official Birthday: Prince Harry attends his first Trooping the Colour. The Eiffel Tower in Paris celebrates its 100th birthday with a spectacular firework display, 800,000 guests and a 25m tall birthday cake!

Sunday June 18

Father's Day. 29°C at Saunton Sands, Devon. It's so hot in the West Country that roads melt in Keynsham, nr Bath, Avon, and Coalpit Heath, nr Bristol.

Monday June 19

Heatwave spreads from Land's End to John O'Groats. The House of Lords beats the House of Commons in the annual Tug-of-War Contest.

Full Moon

Tuesday June 20

It's so hot that jockeys drink water with a teaspoon of salt and sugar as a precaution against heat stroke on the opening day of Royal Ascot. 990 people are rescued from the Soviet cruise liner *Maxim Gorky* after she hits an iceberg deep inside the Arctic Circle.

Wednesday June 21

Longest day of the year. Sun rise 4.43am, sun set 9.22pm. Happy Birthday to Prince William, who is seven today!

Thursday June 22

John Craven reads the news for the last time on the 2926th edition of BBC 1's 'Newsround'.

Friday June 23

A newly-discovered stretch of London's Roman wall, 9.1m long and 10.3m high, goes on show near the Minories and the Tower of London.

Saturday June 24

A 30km oil slick slithers along Rhode Island on the east coast of the US and the surf turns orange after a Greek tanker *World Prodigy* runs aground and spills 2,954,900 litres of fuel.

Sunday June 25

Russell Byers, from Mapperley, Nottingham, becomes National Scrabble Champion winning four games in a row with a score of 2075.

Monday June 26

Opening day of the 103rd Wimbledon Lawn Tennis Championships. The fountain in St James' Park, London, is turned off because of the water shortage.

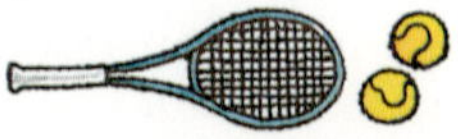

Tuesday June 27

The Princess of Wales finishes second in the mothers' race at Prince William's school sports day at the Richmond Sports Ground, London.

Wednesday June 28

Be careful not to pick the *Gladiolus illyricus*, which is flowering in the New Forest! It is one of a rare species that is pollinated by butterflies and protected by the 1981 Wildlife and Countryside Act.

Thursday June 29

The Juno Astronaut Hotline opens in London to find the first British spaceperson, who will be trained in Star City, nr Moscow, before taking off for *Mir*, the orbiting Soviet space station.

Friday June 30

Peter Wells, from Beeston, Beds, arrives in London just before 2am, having cycled 640km from Edinburgh in 17hrs 48mins. Despite two punctures, he knocks over an hour off the previous record set in 1965.

Happy Birthday

The office of Lord Mayor of London is 800 years old
Ely Cathedral is 800 years old
The gold sovereign is 500 years old
The French Revolution is 200 years old
The Clifton Suspension Bridge, Bristol, is 125 years old
The Eiffel Tower is 100 years old
The Moulin Rouge is 100 years old
The RSPB is 100 years old
The Savoy Hotel, London, is 100 years old
The Singer electric sewing machine is 100 years old
The Brownies are 75 years old
Winnie the Pooh is 75 years old
The Save the Children Fund is 70 years old
Tintin is 60 years old
NATO is 40 years old
The Hovercraft is 30 years old
The Barbie doll is 30 years old
Postcodes are 30 years old
The Red Arrows are 25 years old

July

Saturday
July 1

Happy 28th Birthday to the Princess of Wales! 198 cyclists begin the 3255km Tour de France in Luxembourg.

Sunday
July 2

Mr Eppo Harbrink Numan lands on the Isle of Mull, off the west coast of Scotland, after flying from Rotterdam in his microlight aircraft on his 8000km journey across the Atlantic to New York, via Iceland and Greenland.

New Moon

Monday
July 3

Astronomers get out their telescopes to inspect the surface of Saturn's giant moon, Titan, which lights up in the night sky when it passes just in front of the bright star 28 Sagittarii at 11.41pm.

Tuesday
July 4

American Independence Day. The Post Office unveils a £1,500,000 computer system called TATOM (Tracking and Tracing of Overseas Mail). It will use bar codes to track mail all over the world.

Wednesday
July 5

A lightweight Japanese vehicle, made of plastic and aluminium and sponsored by Honda, wins the Shell Mileage Marathon at Silverstone. It looks like a horizontal teardrop and has an average fuel consumption of 7,485km per gallon.

Thursday
July 6

Violent thunderstorms sweep across the Midlands. Lightning strikes the Australian flagpole at Edgbaston, Birmingham, as rain stops play in the third Test Match.

Friday
July 7

More than 100 hot-air balloons manage to take off at the start of Southampton Balloon Festival, although there are floods all over the south and west of England after torrential rain.

Saturday
July 8

151 vessels sail down the river Thames from Tower Bridge for the start of the Cutty Sark Tall Ships Race from Harwich to Hamburg.

Sunday
July 9

Boris Becker (West Germany) wins the men's singles title at Wimbledon, beating Stefan Edberg 6–0, 7–6, 6–4. Steffi Graf (West Germany) becomes the women's singles champion, beating Martina Navratilova 6–2, 6–7, 6–1.

Monday
July 10

Volunteers at the Orkney Seal Rescue Centre work day and night to save seals as a deadly distemper virus returns to the North Sea. Four pups called Flo, Flipper, Alex and Paris are fed with minced herring and porridge oats.

Tuesday
July 11

Bodelwyddan Castle, Clwyd, Wales, is named Museum of the Year by National Heritage. Vicki Keith (Canada), swims the English Channel in 23hrs 33mins using butterfly stroke.

July

Named in honour of Julius Caesar. Also known as 'the yellow month' (Gaelic) and 'the month of the mid-summer moon' (Anglo Saxon).

The Eiffel Tower

The Eiffel Tower was commissioned by the French Government in 1889 to celebrate the 100th anniversary of the French Revolution. Designed by Gustave Eiffel, it took 18 months to build and cost 7,799,401 francs 31 centimes. At nearly 300m high, it was the tallest building in the world for more than 40yrs. Materials included 6,795,000kg of wrought iron and 2,500,000 rivets. Altogether there were 1792 steps to the top. Reactions to the tallest tower were somewhat mixed—from 'Useless!' to 'Monstrous!' to 'More like a tragic lampstand!'.

However, this year, more than 5,000,000 people will visit the Eiffel Tower and there is a Post Office on the first platform which will stamp more than 300,000 cards and letters. The tower needs painting every 7 years with 40 tonnes of special 'Eiffel Brown' paint.

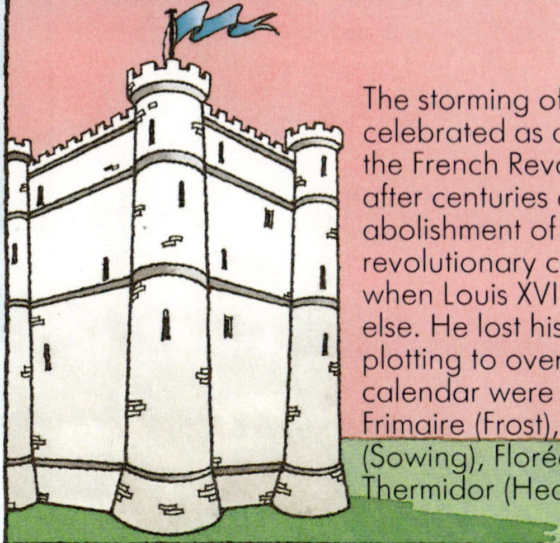

French Revolution

The storming of the Bastille, a royal fortress in Paris, on July 14, 1789, is celebrated as a national holiday in France each year. A turning point in the French Revolution, when ordinary citizens and peasants seized power after centuries of starvation, injustice and royal oppression, it led to the abolishment of the monarchy and the birth of a new Republic. A revolutionary calendar was introduced in 1792, Year 1 of the Republic, when Louis XVI lost the title of 'King' and became 'Citizen', like everybody else. He lost his head early the next year when he was found guilty of plotting to overthrow the Revolution. The new months of the revolutionary calendar were called Vendémiaire (Grape harvest), Brumaire (Mist), Frimaire (Frost), Nivôse (Snow), Pluviôse (Rain), Ventôse (Winds), Germinal (Sowing), Floréal (Blossom), Prairial (Haymaking), Messidor (Harvesting), Thermidor (Heat) and Fructidor (Fruits).

July 4 PO issues 5 new stamps celebrating Industrial Archaeology

Wednesday July 12

Europe's largest civil communications satellite, *Olympus*, is launched from French Guiana while Judy Leden, from Derbyshire, takes off from Dover to become the first woman to cross the English Channel by hang glider.

Thursday July 13

Portia, a black Berkshire sow that belongs to the Right Rev. Robert Runcie, Archbishop of Canterbury, wins first prize in the interbreed pig championship at the Kent Agricultural Show, Maidstone.

Friday July 14

There are huge celebrations in Paris today to mark the 200th anniversary of the French Revolution. 5200 soldiers and 300 armoured vehicles take part in a military parade down the Champs Elysées—accompanied by 250 planes and helicopters.

Saturday July 15

Police capture a 3.6m python called Boris in Cumberland Road, Southampton.

Sunday July 16

Shellfish harvesting is banned at Morlaix, Brittany, after an invasion of poisonous seaweed and jellyfish.

Monday July 17

The £340,000,000 B2 Stealth bomber makes its maiden flight over the Mojave Desert, California, USA. Typhoon Gordon roars into Hong Kong and injures 30 people.

Tuesday July 18

Mr D.W. Smith, from Bolton, Lancs, wins a gold medal for his collection of 110 different gooseberries at the Royal Horticultural Show, London.

Full Moon

Wednesday July 19

Two lanes of the M6 in Staffordshire, between junctions 12 and 13, melt in the heat.

Thursday July 20

It's the 20th anniversary of the day the American astronauts Neil Armstrong and Buzz Aldrin, the first men ever to do so walked on the moon. They left behind them the Laser Ranging Retro-reflector, which shows that the moon is moving 3.8cm away from the Earth each year.

30°C in Leeds

Friday July 21

Comedian Ken Dodd, in court on charges of not paying enough income tax, admits that he kept £336,000 in the attic as a 'nest egg'.

Saturday July 22

There is a ladybird plague on the South Coast because of the mild winter and long, hot summer.

Sunday July 23

Greg Lemond (US) wins the Tour de France in Paris by 8 seconds, with an average speed of 54.4kph.

Monday July 24

Prime Minister, Mrs Thatcher, reshuffles her Cabinet and appoints John Major (46) Foreign Secretary. Britain's first space school is launched at Sevenoaks, Kent.

Tuesday July 25

Mr Sean Shannon, of Oxford, becomes the world's fastest talker after reciting the 260-word 'To Be Or Not To Be' speech from Hamlet in 26.8secs.

Wednesday July 26

Liverpool's Albert Dock comes top in the 'Come to Britain' Awards sponsored by the British Tourist Authority. The Rev. Robin Blount is appointed the first Chaplain of the Channel Tunnel.

Thursday July 27

American Tom Gentry wins the Virgin Atlantic Challenge trophy after crossing the Atlantic in the record time of 62hrs 7mins 47secs in his 33.5m speedboat *Gentry Eagle* from New York to the Bishop Rock lighthouse, Isles of Scilly.

Friday July 28

The King's Troop of the Royal Horse Artillery will not be at the Royal Tournament, Earl's Court, this year because of an outbreak of equine flu. 25 horses have been ill and are in quarantine.

Saturday July 29

Cuban athlete Javier Sotomayor (21) breaks the high jump record at the Caribbean athletics championships in Puerto Rico with a jump of 2.44m.

Sunday July 30

Rain falls for the first time in weeks all over England and Wales. There are thunderstorms on Humberside and in Birmingham. Scotland Yard is baffled by reports of UFOs over London and the South East last night.

Monday July 31

The London Weather Centre has recorded 278 hours of sunshine this month, beating the 1976 July record by three hours! More than 2,000,000 tourists visit the UK this July—an 8% increase on the same month last year.

*Top Ten UK LPs**

1 A New Flame—Simply Red
2 Ten Good Reasons—Jason Donovan
3 Anything For You—Gloria Estefan
4 Enjoy Yourself—Kylie Minogue
5 Like A Prayer—Madonna
6 The Raw and The Cooked—Fine Young Cannibals
7 When The World Knows Your Name—Deacon Blue
8 Don't Be Cruel—Bobby Brown
9 Club Classics Vol One—Soul II Soul
10 . . . But Seriously—Phil Collins

* according to the *New Musical Express*

*Top Ten Box Office Films**

1 Indiana Jones and The Last Crusade
2 Batman
3 Rainman
4 Naked Gun
5 Licence To Kill
6 Who Framed Roger Rabbit?
7 Twins
8 Lethal Weapon
9 Back To The Future Part 2
10 Dead Poet's Society

* compiled by MRIB

August

Tuesday August 1

Snow falls in Switzerland and blocks Alpine passes. A six-nation dog-sled team leaves King George Island to trek across Antarctica from west to east—the longest and most difficult route.

New Moon

Wednesday August 2

Thousands of people are evacuated from the French Riviera as forest fires are fanned by strong winds.

Thursday August 3

A 14m Sei whale is stranded on rocks near St Mawes on the Roseland Peninsula in Cornwall.

Friday August 4

Lidana, a rare Malaysian tapir born on Tuesday at Port Lympne Zoo Park, nr Hythe, Kent, shows off her spots and stripes. They will disappear when she is about 10 months old.

Saturday August 5

The Savoy Hotel in London celebrates its 100th birthday with a grand party and firework display. 153 yachts sail down the Solent at the start of the 973km Fastnet Race.

Sunday August 6

Kate Goodale (32) from the USA, becomes the 364th person to swim across the English Channel, crossing the 34.5km from Dover to Cap Gris Nez in 11hrs 53mins.

Monday August 7

A 1.8m reticulated python called Buster is found in a lavatory in a block of flats in Prince's Gate, London.

Tuesday August 8

The European Space Agency's *Hipparcus* satellite, which will measure distances between the stars, is launched on board the *Ariane 4* space rocket from French Guiana. Sid and Pippa become the parents of Puck, the first Hartmann's Mountain Zebra to be born at London Zoo for 26yrs!

Wednesday August 9

Greenpeace's new ship *Rainbow Warrior* sails up the Thames for a week's visit to Britain. A 60cm monitor lizard is captured by the police and taken to London Zoo after it bites an Alsatian dog in East St, Walworth.

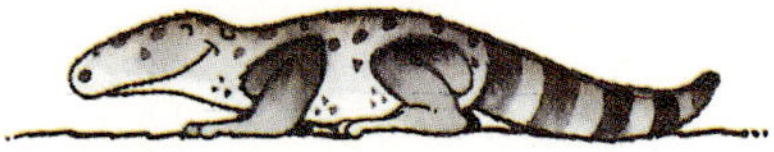

Thursday August 10

Heavy rain in the south of England and Wales. 2cms fall in central London, making it the wettest day for almost 5 months.

Friday August 11

The £26,000,000 budget film *Batman* opens in London. It's the first Certificate 12 film, which means that children under 11 can't see it—even if they're with an adult.

Saturday August 12

Best night of the year to see the famous Perseid meteor shower! 100th Amateur Athletics Championships are held in Birmingham.

Sunday August 13	Sean Yates (28) from Forest Row, Sussex, becomes the first Briton to win the Tour of Belgium cycle race, finishing 1 second ahead of Frans Maasen of Holland.
Monday August 14	A 145kph tornado devastates Butlins' holiday camp at Pwllheli, North Wales, causing £2,000,000 damage.
Tuesday August 15	Adrian Moorhouse sets a new 100m world breaststroke record of 1min 1.49secs in a heat at the European Championship in Bonn.
Wednesday August 16	Two Army cadets set a new British record when they abseil 202m down the cooling towers at Littlebrook Power Station, Kent.
Thursday August 17	Total eclipse of the moon in Britain between 2.20am and 3.20am. Qantas jumbo jet *The City of Canberra* arrives in Sydney, Australia, after flying non-stop from London in 20hrs 9mins and setting a new long distance record. Full Moon
Friday August 18	Arturo Barrios, from Mexico, sets a new 10,000m world record in Berlin with a time of 27mins 8.23secs.

August

Named in honour of the Roman Emperor Augustus, whose lucky month it was. Also known as 'harvest month' and 'weed month'.

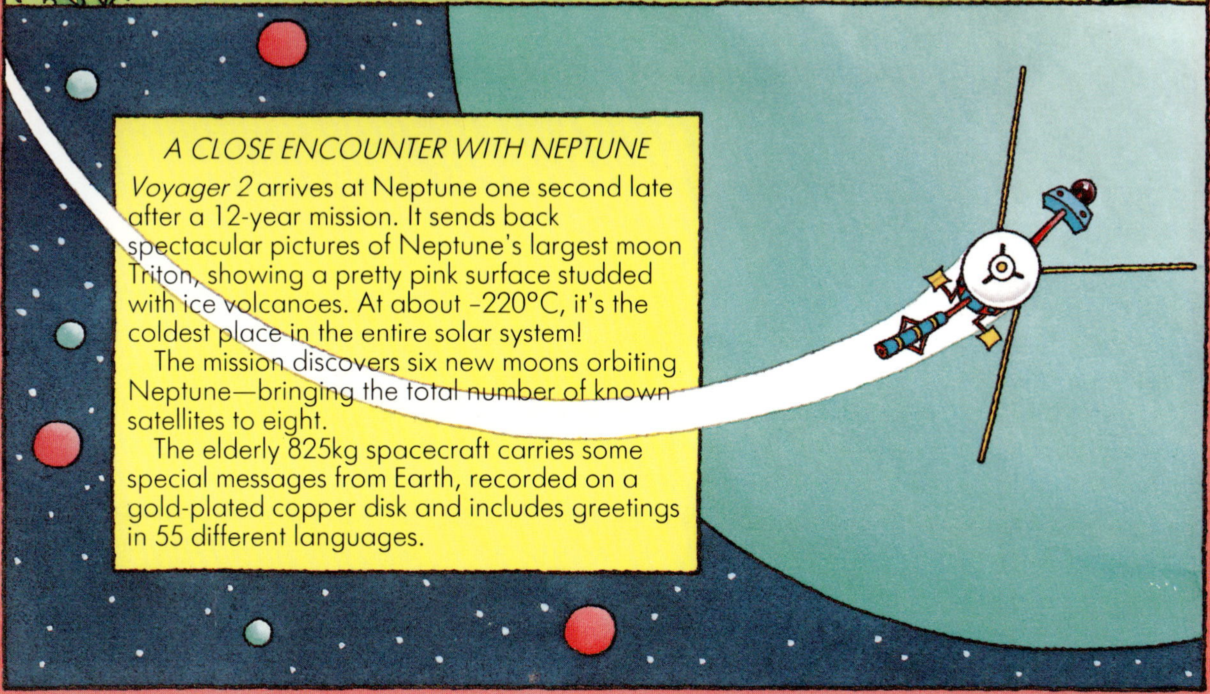

A CLOSE ENCOUNTER WITH NEPTUNE

Voyager 2 arrives at Neptune one second late after a 12-year mission. It sends back spectacular pictures of Neptune's largest moon Triton, showing a pretty pink surface studded with ice volcanoes. At about -220°C, it's the coldest place in the entire solar system!

The mission discovers six new moons orbiting Neptune—bringing the total number of known satellites to eight.

The elderly 825kg spacecraft carries some special messages from Earth, recorded on a gold-plated copper disk and includes greetings in 55 different languages.

Saturday
August 19

John Evans, of Fforest-fach, Swansea, celebrates his 112th birthday.

Sunday
August 20

Blacksmith Jamie Reeves, who weighs 146kg and comes from Sheffield, wins the Strongest Man in the World title in San Sebastian, Spain.

30.4°C at Coltishall, nr Norwich

Monday
August 21

Flour millers Bartley Mill, of Tunbridge Wells, Kent, produce 13 loaves of bread from a field of wheat in 29mins 40secs and set a new world record—with the help of a microwave!

Tuesday
August 22

6000 houses in Didcot, Milton and Sutton Courtenay, Oxfordshire, are blacked out after a squirrel bites through an 11,000 volt power cable.

Wednesday
August 23

2,000,000 people in the Baltic States of the Soviet Union demonstrate their nationalism by holding hands and forming a chain that stretches 595km through Estonia, Latvia and Lithuania.

Thursday
August 24

Jane Webber lands at Plymouth in her 12.8m monohull *Tilley Endurable*, after leaving Halifax, Nova Scotia, 27 days ago, and becomes the first Canadian woman to cross the Atlantic single-handed.

Friday
August 25

After a 12-year, 7 billion kilometre flight from Earth, *Voyager 2* space probe is only one second late when it passes Neptune early today.

Saturday
August 26

Clansmen set off at 8am to march nearly 13km for the opening of the Highland Gatherings and Games at Blairbeg Park, Drumnadrochit, Inverness-shire at 1pm.

Sunday
August 27

Mission Control throws a huge party to celebrate *Voyager 2*'s successful flight to Neptune.

Monday
August 28

Bank Holiday. Bog Snorkelling Championships are held at Llanwrtyd Wells, Powys. World Pitchfork Championship is held at the Whitbread Hop Farm, Beltring, Kent.

Tuesday
August 29

The British Toy and Hobby Manufacturers' Association announces the use of a new Lion safety symbol.

Wednesday
August 30

Lisa West (5), from Raynes Park, London, is named the 32nd Miss Pears at the Savoy Hotel in London, beating 23,000 other entrants.

New Moon—the second this month!

Thursday
August 31

Uppark, South Harting, Sussex, one of the finest 17th century houses in Britain, is gutted by fire. Restoration starts immediately.

September

Friday September 1	From today, children sitting in the backs of cars must wear seat belts. Oyster smacks race on the river Thames at Gravesend, Kent, to celebrate the opening of the oyster season.
Saturday September 2	24 yachts leave the Solent for Uruguay at the start of the 53,000km Whitbread Round the World Race.
Sunday September 3	50 years ago today World War II began. A bronze statue of the 'Unknown Airman' is unveiled on Plymouth Hoe. Dr John Sykes wins *The Times/Collins Dictionaries* Crossword Championship for the 9th time. He completes 4 crosswords in an average time of $7\frac{1}{2}$ mins each.
Monday September 4	The British maxi yacht *Rothmans* takes the lead in the Whitbread Round the World race in the Bay of Biscay.
Tuesday September 5	46 people are rescued from a Boeing 737, which disappeared in the Amazon jungle on Sept. 2.
Wednesday September 6	Soviet cosmonauts Aleksandr Serebrov and Aleksandr Viktorenko blast off in a Soyuz TM8 space craft to join the orbiting space station *Mir* for 6 months.
Thursday September 7	Prince Harry (4yrs $11\frac{3}{4}$ months) misses his first day at Wetherby School, Notting Hill Gate, because of a viral infection.
Friday September 8	United Nations International Literacy year is launched in New York. 150 firemen and 20 fire engines fight a huge blaze sweeping across more than 36 hectares of the New Forest, Hants. The two Soviet cosmonauts who left Earth on Wednesday make a manual link-up with space station *Mir* after the automatic docking system fails.
Saturday September 9	Thamesday in London: a 23m inflatable dragon and a large Origami paper boat take part in the floating pageant.
Sunday September 10	Britain's show jumping team (Rodney Powell, Lorna Clarke, Virginia Leng and Ian Stark) wins the gold medal at the European Three-Day Event Championships at Burghley, Lincs.
Monday September 11	River police use special radar traps to catch people breaking the new 9.6kph speed limit on the Norfolk Broads. Prince Harry starts school (mornings only) and makes a model elephant.
Tuesday September 12	Ministry of Agriculture issues a cucumber downy-mildew warning after two outbreaks in Sussex and Cambridgeshire.

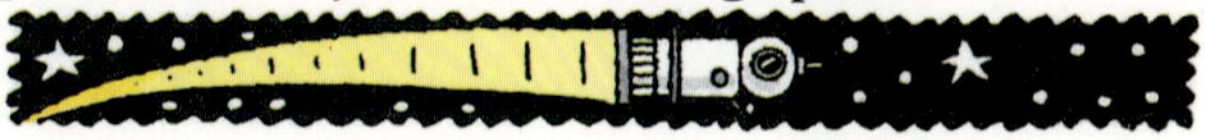

Wednesday September 13	The first World Congress of Herpetology (study of reptiles) is held at the University of Kent, Canterbury.
Thursday September 14	Treasure hunters begin raising gold bars and coins from the wreck of the steamer *Central America*, which sank off the coast of South Carolina, USA, in 1857 with about 3 tonnes of gold on board. 
Friday September 15	The drought in the south west of England officially ends after 7.6cm rain falls. The famous St Leger horse race at Doncaster is postponed after part of the course subsides: it will be run at Ayr on Sept. 23. Full Moon 
Saturday September 16	Annual Day of Love and Friendship in Colombia, S. America. Farm Watch is launched in Wales to fight sheep rustling.
Sunday September 17	Hurricane Hugo hits the NE Caribbean at 225kph. British Footpaths and Farming Day 1989: angry members of the Ramblers' Association lace up their boots and protest about the disappearing footpath.
Monday September 18	A special £15,000 tortoise tunnel is being built under a new motorway between Toulon and St Tropez in the south of France.  
Tuesday September 19	A two-tone brown teddy bear, made by Steiff in Germany in 1920, is sold for £55,000 at Sotheby's, London. 
Wednesday September 20	A £110,000,000, 45,720 tonne, vessel—a combination oil rig and tanker—is named *Seillean* (Gaelic for 'Bee') at the Harland and Wolff shipyard in Belfast.
Thursday September 21	A granite memorial to Wing Commander Guy Gibson, who led the 617 Dam Buster squadron in World War II, is unveiled in Porthleven, Cornwall.
Friday September 22	Hurricane Hugo, the worst storm to hit the US mainland since Hurricane Hazel in 1954, arrives in Charleston, S. Carolina, USA at 222kph. Buildings are flattened, the roof of City Hall is blown off and the sea is swept 16km inland.
Saturday September 23	10th World Open Leek Championship and the World's Heaviest Onion Challenge are held in Ashington, Northumberland. 
Sunday September 24	National Breakfast Day in France: the French Health Education committee launches a campaign to promote bacon and eggs. 
Monday September 25	John McGregor, the new Secretary of State for Education and Science, has school dinner (salad) at Redenhall Dove School, Norfolk.

Tuesday September 26

Javelin thrower Tessa Sanderson launches the 1989 'Jump Rope (Skip) for Heart' campaign to encourage skipping.

Wednesday September 27

Paris, a common seal, says goodbye to the Orkney Seal Rescue Centre after recovering from phocine distemper virus, and splashes out to sea.

Thursday September 28

Green Consumer Day. The Australian cricket team arrives back in Sydney after winning the Ashes: they are given the keys to the City by the Lord Mayor.

Friday September 29

Lava bubbles out of Mount Etna for the second day running: it's the highest and most active volcano in Europe.

New Moon 

Saturday September 30

Jewish New Year (AM 5750). It's been the warmest September in Oxford for 40 years and the driest September in Durham since 1898!

September

This was the seventh month of the year in the old Roman calendar when the year used to start in March. Also known as the 'month of reaping', 'barley month' and 'holy month'.

Mir

The Soviet Union space station *Mir*, which means *Peace*, was launched on February 20 1986. Cosmonauts Aleksandr Serebrov and Aleksandr Viktorenko start a 6-month visit to *Mir* on Sept. 8. The walls, floor and ceiling of *Mir*'s work compartment are painted different colours so that the cosmonauts know which way up they are. The men have been trained to work in space by practising under 5m of water in a special swimming pool at Star City, Moscow. There are 2 cabins—each with a small desk, a foldaway seat and a sleeping bag fixed upright to the wall.

September 5 PO issues 4 new stamps to mark the 150th anniversary of the Royal Microscopical Society

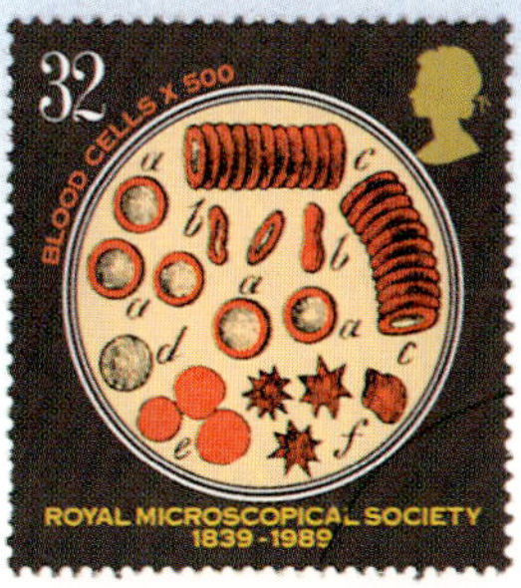

October

Sunday October 1
The Pearly King and Queen go to a special Pearly Harvest Festival at St Martin-in-the-Fields Church, London. Pakistan is formally re-admitted to the Commonwealth as the 49th member state.

Monday October 2
7000 East German refugees pour across the border into West Germany. The East German government accuses them of treason.

Tuesday October 3
The first crime for more than 80yrs on the island of Foula in the Shetlands is reported to the police after a Land Rover is vandalised.

Wednesday October 4
The Red Arrows celebrate their 25th anniversary at their base at Scampton, Lincs, with air display teams from France, Switzerland, Spain, Italy and Portugal. Launch of a £250,000 appeal to save the Avebury Circles in Wiltshire.

Thursday October 5
His Holiness Tenzin Gyatso, Dalai Lama of Tibet, is awarded the Nobel peace prize.

23.2°C at Faversham, Kent

Friday October 6
70 tonnes of chocolate are destroyed in a fire at Cadbury's factory in Marlbrook, nr Leominster, Hereford and Worcester. One of Britain's first £1 bank notes, issued in 1797, is sold for £18,700.

Saturday October 7
100 bands take part in the Boosey and Hawkes National Brass Band Championships at the Albert Hall, London. It is won by the Desford Colliery Caterpillar Band from the North Midlands. Mount Etna, is still erupting. The airport in Sicily is closed after ash and black dust cover the runways.

Sunday October 8
Peter Short, from Scotland, wins the 25th World Conker Championship at Ashton, nr Oundle, Cambs.

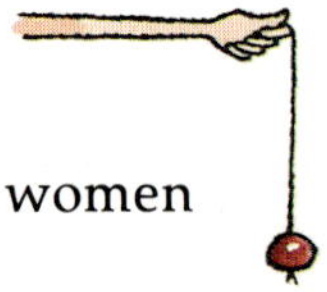

Monday October 9
Jewish Day of Atonement (Yom Kippur). 14 men and 2 women begin tests at the RAF's Institute of Aviation Medicine, Farnborough, to determine who will be the first British astronaut to join a special mission to *Mir*, the orbiting Soviet space station.

Tuesday October 10
An unexploded World War II bomb is found near roadworks at Junction 2 on the M25, at Dartford, Kent.

Wednesday October 11
A dolphin, stranded on the beach at Malltraeth, Anglesey, is rescued by an RAF helicopter and taken out to sea in a net.

Thursday October 12
First National History Day. Archaeologists discover the remains of the Globe Theatre, nr Southwark Bridge, London, where many of Shakespeare's most famous plays were first performed.

October

This was the eighth month in the old Roman calendar when the year started in March. It has also been known as 'wine month' and 'month of the winter moon'.

The Plymouth Sound Seahorse

The seahorse is a member of the pipefish family. Its proper name is *Hippocampus ramulosus* and it usually lives in warm waters like the Mediterranean. It is more than 30yrs since a seahorse has been found off the south coast of England. This one, found lurking amongst eel grass off Drake's Island in Plymouth Sound, is about 110mm long, with a curly tail and a tiny mouth at the end of a bony snout. In fact, it looks more like a small dragon or chess piece than a fish. It is taken to live in Plymouth Aquarium where it joins other warm-water species like the marbled electric ray and the triggerfish.

The female seahorse lays her eggs in a pouch under the male's tail. He takes care of them until they hatch.

A distant and highly camouflaged branch of the family (Phyllopteryx) lives in Australia and pretends to be rockweed.

Daily Bugle

WATER FLEA TO BE USED IN BATTLE AGAINST NORFOLK BROADS ALGAE

The Reporter

OIL SPILL AT US ANTARCTIC BASE COULD CONTAMINATE SNOW AND ICE FOR A CENTURY

Chit-Chat

NORTHANTS NUNS LOCK THEMSELVES IN HENHOUSE TO SAVE 5,000 CHICKENS FROM SLAUGHTER

Scoop

JAPANESE BUY THE ROCKEFELLER CENTRE, NEW YORK, FOR £35,000,000

October 17 PO issues 5 new stamps to celebrate the Lord Mayor's Show in London

Friday
October 13

Happy 64th Birthday to Prime Minister, Margaret Thatcher. Watch out for computer virus Friday the Thirteenth!

Saturday
October 14

The Battle of Hastings 1066. William, Duke of Normandy, with 5000 Knights from France, Flanders, Spain and Italy, defeated King Harold. TV journalist Kate Adie is awarded the freedom of her home town, Sunderland, for her coverage of Chinese pro-democracy demonstrations in Tiananmen Square.

Full Moon

Sunday
October 15

Bert Waller, from Andover, catches a 5.6kg conger eel off Portugal and becomes England's champion sea angler.

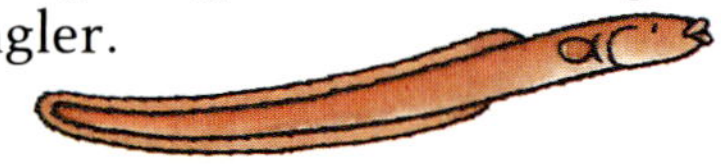

Monday
October 16

The Convention on International Trade in Endangered Species in Lausanne, Switzerland, votes to ban all trade in ivory.

Tuesday
October 17

A major earthquake in San Francisco (the worst since 1906) measures 6.9 on the Richter Scale, destroying part of the Bay Bridge and a 1.5km section of the double-decker Nimitz Freeway.

Wednesday
October 18

St Luke's Day. US space shuttle *Atlantis* is launched from Cape Canaveral, Florida, carrying the space craft *Galileo* at the start of its 6-year journey to Jupiter. A sea horse (*Hippocampus ramulosus*) is found by the research vessel *Sepia* in shallow water off Drake's Island in Plymouth Sound.

Thursday
October 19

Three powerful aftershocks (two of them registering 5 on the Richter Scale) follow the major earthquake in San Francisco on Tuesday. Five earthquakes, one measuring 6.1 on the Richter Scale, rock northern China.

Friday
October 20

129kph winds sweep the south and south west of England, tearing down power lines.

Saturday
October 21

Trafalgar Day. An elephant called Arusha recovers at the Animal Health Trust, Newmarket, Suffolk, after having a tooth filled. The operation took five hours and used 3 months supply of filling!

Sunday
October 22

The worst storms since the hurricane of October 1987 sweep southern England, Scotland and N. Ireland.

Monday
October 23

US space shuttle *Atlantis* lands safely at Edwards Air Force Base, California, after launching spacecraft *Galileo* towards Venus on the first leg of a 6-year journey to the planet Jupiter. The craft is already more than 1,609,000km away from Earth, moving at 14,500kph!

Tuesday October 24

The Queen starts the XIVth Commonwealth Games relay from the front of Buckingham Palace this afternoon.

Wednesday October 25

Skyscrapers sway in San Francisco during more aftershocks following the major earthquake eight days ago. The biggest tremor measures 4.2 on the Richter Scale.

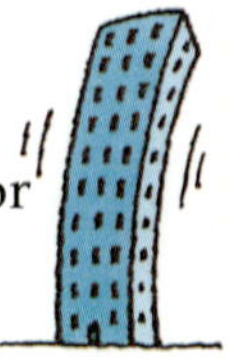

Thursday October 26

Nigel Lawson resigns as Chancellor of the Exchequer and is replaced by John Major. Stirling Moss's Formula 1 racing car, which won the Dutch and Portuguese Grand Prix in 1958, is sold at Brook's car auction in London for £1,595,000.

Friday October 27

National Boys' Club Week. The Children's Bill which will radically reform the law concerning the upbringing, care and protection of children, is given an unopposed third reading in the House of Commons.

Saturday October 28

Torrential rain and gales all over the country. A gust of 162.5kph is recorded at Portland Bill, Dorset. 10.4cms rain falls at Moel Cynnedd, Powys. Bad weather in the Southern Ocean as the Whitbread Round The World fleet leaves Uruguay for Fremantle, Australia (11,681km).

Sunday October 29

Storms in South Wales and the west of England. British Summer Time ends at 2am. A Briton, Paul Davies-Hale, wins the Chicago Marathon in 2hrs 11mins 25secs.

New Moon

Monday October 30

A model of Buckingham Palace, made of 43,761 Lego bricks, goes on display at the Royal Britain Exhibition in the City of London.

Tuesday October 31

Hallowe'en. *The Flying Scotsman* leaves Sydney for Britain after a 15-month, 48,000km tour of Australia.

1989 Coin Collection

The gold sovereign was created 500 years ago when, in 1489, King Henry VII told the Royal Mint in the Tower of London to produce 'a new money of gold'. The new coin, the largest ever issued in England, was worth 20 shillings. This year, to celebrate the anniversary, the Royal Mint issues a set of four gold coins: five pounds (39.94g), double sovereign (15.98g), sovereign (7.98g) and half-sovereign (3.99g).

Other special coins this year include commemorative £2 coins to mark the 300th anniversary of the Bill of Rights and the Scottish Claim of Right, which established Parliament as the centre of political power in Britain, and a medal to celebrate the 800th anniversary of the Lord Mayor of the City of London.

November

Wednesday November 1

The Government launches a campaign to persuade motor cyclists, horse riders and cyclists to wear glow-in-the-dark clothes.

Thursday November 2

A British Airways DC10, carrying the Duchess of York and 191 other passengers, flies on safely to Houston, Texas, USA, from Gatwick, after being struck by lightning off the west coast of Scotland.

Friday November 3

Roger Southwell, of Watermill Farm, Northwold, Norfolk, digs up more than 200 tonnes of potatoes in less than 4hrs and claims a new world record.

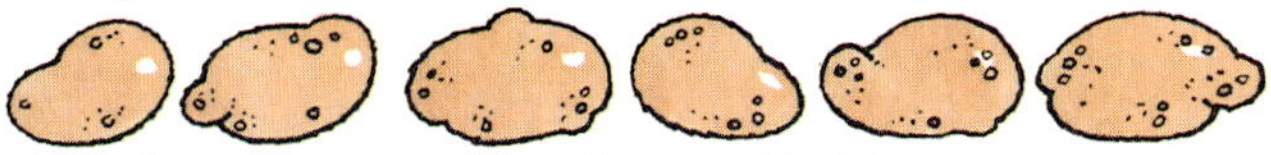

Saturday November 4

There are pro-democracy demonstrations all over E. Germany, with a 1,0000,000-strong rally in E. Berlin.

Sunday November 5

Bonfire Night. Roger Collings, from Hereford, wins the 92km London to Brighton veteran car run in a 1903 Mercedes in just over 2hrs.

First snow of the winter in Snowdonia

Monday November 6

Work starts on the first aqueduct to be built in Britain for 50yrs—it will carry the Grand Union Canal over a new road at Milton Keynes.

Tuesday November 7

A new world record price for stamps is set at Harmers, London, when a block of 36 unused Penny Blacks fetch £308,000.

Wednesday November 8

Linda Pritchard, of Hanwell, Middlesex, relaxes in Greenwich after running 6436km through England, Wales, Scotland and N. Ireland—the equivalent of a marathon every day!

Thursday November 9

E. Germany opens its borders for the first time and allows citizens to leave the country freely.

Friday November 10

Goodbye to the Berlin Wall, which has divided the city for 28 years! Thousands of people dance and celebrate on top of it as the bulldozers move in.

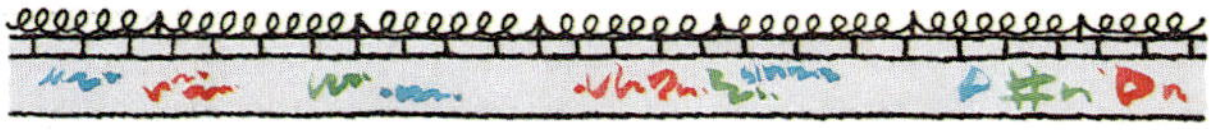

Saturday November 11

Lord Mayor's Show in London. The new Lord Mayor, Sir Hugh Bidwell, leaves Guildhall with a procession of 20 coaches and more than 50 floats on his way to be sworn in at the Law Courts.

Sunday November 12

Remembrance Sunday. Helen Sharman, Gordon Brooks, Timothy Mace and Clive Smith, one of whom will become the first British astronaut on a mission to the orbiting space station *Mir*, leave for final tests in the Soviet Union.

November

This was the ninth month of the Roman calendar when the year started in March. The old Saxon name was 'wind-monath'—wind month. The old Dutch name was 'slaght-maand'—slaughter month.

THE BERLIN WALL

At the end of World War II, Berlin, the former capital of Germany, was divided between Britain, US, France and the Soviet Union. The three sectors occupied by the Western Powers became known as West Berlin with the fourth section, controlled by the Soviet Union, known as East Berlin. During the years after the war, thousands of East German citizens fled across the border from communist East Berlin to seek a new life in the West. On August 13, 1961, to stem the flood of refugees, the East German government built a huge barbed wire barrier across the city, completely surrounding West Berlin. The barrier was later replaced by a 2m high concrete wall, topped with barbed wire and dotted with observation turrets. The official crossing points were manned by armed guards. Despite this, refugees from East Berlin still tried to escape to the West by crossing the Wall and in 1970 its height was raised to 3m. The demolition of the wall led to the reunification of Germany.

*Top Ten Names**

1	Elizabeth	1	James
2	Charlotte	2	William
3	Alice	3	Alexander
4	Emily	4	Edward
5	Victoria	5	Thomas
6	Emma	6	Charles
7	Sophie	7	John
8	Alexandra	8	George
9	Sarah	9	David
10	Lucy	10	Robert

* according to *The Times* newspaper

November 14 PO issues new Christmas stamps

Monday November 13
Dense fog in central and southern England. The BBC's annual 'Children In Need' appeal raises £21,671,931.

Full Moon 

Tuesday November 14
Happy 41st Birthday to the Prince of Wales! The Post Office issues five new Christmas stamps, celebrating the 800th anniversary of Ely Cathedral. Four of the five cost 1p extra, which goes to charity.

Wednesday November 15
850 athletes from 34 nations compete in the eighth Asian Championships in Delhi.

Thursday November 16
50,000,000 bottles of Beaujolais Nouveau are sent all over the world. In Japan, the first bottles to arrive cost 19,600 yen (£86).

Friday November 17
Rudolf Nureyev (51) dances with the Kirov Ballet in Leningrad for the first time since he defected to the West in 1961.

Saturday November 18
Bob Monkhouse switches on the Christmas lights at Ampthill, Beds. Special £99 day trip charter flights leave Gatwick airport for Germany to collect chunks of the Berlin Wall.

Sunday November 19
Beginning of National Talking Newspaper Week. 190 competitors start the 5-day RAC Rally from Wollaton Park, Nottingham.

Monday November 20
The Queen and the Duke of Edinburgh celebrate their 42nd wedding anniversary. The United Nations General Assembly adopts an international treaty on children's rights known as the Convention on the Rights of the Child.

Tuesday November 21
State Opening of Parliament: proceedings in the House of Commons are televised for the first time.

Wednesday November 22
US space shuttle *Discovery* blasts off from Cape Canaveral, Florida, tonight to deploy a secret spy satellite.

Thursday November 23
Pentii Airikkala and Ronan McNamee win the RAC Rally in Nottingham in a Mitsubishi. The Berlin Wall is selling for $7 (£4.46) per 28gms on 5th Avenue, New York, today!

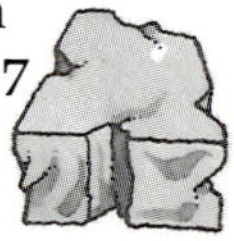

Friday November 24
The second leg of the Whitbread Round the World Race ends in Fremantle, Australia. The New Zealand ketch *Steinlager 2* arrives 1½ hrs ahead of the rest after sailing 12,309km across the Southern Ocean from Uruguay.

Saturday November 25
Moscow TV announces that British astronauts Helen Sharman and Timothy Mace have been chosen for the 8-day Juno mission to the orbiting space station *Mir*.

Sunday
November 26

Two long-eared bats are found hibernating at Britain's first purpose-built Bat Cave at Monkton Nature Reserve nr Ramsgate, Kent.

−10.3°C at Grendon Underwood, Bucks

Monday
November 27

John McCarthy, the British journalist who was kidnapped 3½ years ago in Beirut, is 33 today.

Tuesday
November 28

The Duke of Kent, Patron of the Tree Council, plants an oak tree at Blakeley School in Oldbury, the Midlands, to inaugurate National Tree Week.

New Moon

Wednesday
November 29

The Queen unveils a commemorative plaque at Waterman's Hall, London, after being greeted by a Guard of Honour made up of the Bargemaster, 8 Watermen, the Royal Swan Keeper and 5 Swan Uppers.

Thursday
November 30

St Andrew's Day. Picasso's 'Les Noces de Pierrette' is sold for £32,915,360 in a special satellite link-up sale between Paris and Tokyo.

Champions of 1989

Crufts Champion	Potterdale Classic of Moonhill (Cassie)
Inventor of the Year	Roger Drury
Pipe Smoker of the Year	Jeremy Brett
Champion of Champions Pork Sausage Maker	Keith Boxley
Mastermind	Mary Elizabeth Raw
Mum of the Year	Cathy Kerr
Miss World	Aneka Kreglicka (from Poland)
Miss Universe	Angela Visser (from The Netherlands)
Pup of the Year	Louline High Tide (Hilary)
Museum of the Year	Bodelwyddan, Clwyd
Police Action Dog of the Year	Rocky
Choirgirl of the Year	Rhiannon Williams
Choirboy of the Year	Edward Snow
Hotel of the Year	Gidleigh Park, Devon
Toy of the Year	Transformers
Woman of the Year	Patricia Hart
Times Crossword Champion	Dr John Sykes
World Conker Champion	Peter Short
British Marbles Champion	Paddy Graham
Superkid of the Year	Matthew Rollston
Miss Pears	Lisa West
FA Cup Champions	Liverpool
BR Best Station	Templecombe, Somerset
Boss of the Year	Jill Pattison
Scrabble Champion	Russell Byers
Strongest Man in the World	Jamie Reeves

December

Friday December 1

World AIDS Day. Kylie Minogue switches on the Christmas lights in Regent Street, London.

Saturday December 2

Solar Max, a satellite which has been studying the sun for 9yrs, falls out of orbit over the Indian Ocean and burns up as it re-enters Earth's atmosphere.

Sunday December 3

At the end of National Tree Week, 660,000 trees have been planted all over the country—from Mid Yell in Shetland to Lanhydrock in Cornwall.

Monday December 4

A rare 15cm American sparrow is spotted at Weston, on Portland Bill, Dorset, after being blown across the Atlantic by gales.

Tuesday December 5

A French TGV (Train à Grande Vitesse) reaches a speed of 479kph in the Loire Valley and sets a new world record.

Wednesday December 6

The Queen cancels all engagements this afternoon because she has a dose of flu, which is sweeping the country.

Thursday December 7

The 43rd Christmas Tree lights are switched on in Trafalgar Square, London, by Albert Nordengen, Lord Mayor of Oslo.

Friday December 8

Celebrations in Bristol today to mark the 125th birthday of Isambard Kingdom Brunel's Clifton Suspension Bridge.

Saturday December 9

A large lump of stone falls off the 4600-year-old Sphinx of Giza's left hip which had been repaired unsatisfactorily between 1982 and 1987.

Sunday December 10

UN Human Rights Day. Red Alert at Barnsley District General Hospital, W. Yorks, after more than 100 nurses go down with flu. The Royal College of General Practitioners says it's the worst epidemic for 14yrs, with more than 1,000,000 people affected.

Monday December 11

The international dog-sled team, which set off to cross Antarctica from west to east on August 1, reaches the South Pole.

Tuesday December 12

A solid aluminium head (hat size $7\frac{1}{4}$) called PETE (Protective Equipment Test Effigy) is unveiled at the Health and Safety Executive laboratory in Sheffield to test industrial and sports headwear.

Full Moon

Wednesday December 13

Best night of the year to see the Geminid meteor shower! President F.W. de Klerk of S. Africa meets the jailed ANC leader Nelson Mandela for the first time.

Thursday December 14	Car number plate sale at Christie's, London: 1A fetches £160,000, MUS 1C £71,500, B1 LLY £39,600 and 1 OU £24,200.
Friday December 15	Big Ben stops for more than 3 hours at 11.07am, when part of the clock mechanism seizes up.
Saturday December 16	The 16,300km long National Highway that goes round the coast and down the middle of Australia is completed today. It has taken 15yrs to build, and cost more than $12 billion.
Sunday December 17	Hurricane force winds batter the south and west coasts of Britain with a 193kph gust recorded at Falmouth, Cornwall. The St Mary's lighthouse, Isles of Scilly, is washed away.
Monday December 18	NASA postpones the next US space shuttle because of problems on Launch Pad 39A after a 2-yr $50,000,000 renovation. Heavy snow in Wales
Tuesday December 19	The Queen and the Princess Royal go to a special concert at the Albert Hall, London, to mark the 70th anniversary of the Save The Children Fund.

December

This used to be the tenth month in the old Roman Calendar when the year started in March.

In 1989 the Queen sent 2455 Telemessages to people in this country who celebrated their 100th birthdays. The message reads:

> I am delighted to send you my warm congratulations for your 100th birthday together with my best wishes for an enjoyable celebration.
>
> Elizabeth R.

In the year *they* were born, Lord Salisbury was Prime Minister, Queen Victoria (69), had been on the throne for fifty-two years, and the pneumatic bicycle tyre had just been invented.

Daily Trumpet
PINK-FOOTED GEESE FROM ICELAND EAT CARROT CROP

The Herald
EMERGENCY SUPPLIES OF FLU VACCINE FLOWN TO BRITAIN

Sensation
CHUNK OF THE BERLIN WALL GROUND INTO 1,000 THIMBLES

Daily Lemon
FIERCEST STREET-FIGHTING IN EUROPE SINCE WORLD WAR II AS PRO-DEMOCRACY MOVEMENT OVERTHROWS CEAUCESCU REGIME IN ROMANIA

Wednesday
December 20

Thunderstorms, heavy rain and flash floods sweep southern England. The Royal Marines are drafted in after Sidmouth, Dawlish, and Budleigh Salterton, Devon, are cut off by high tides.

Thursday
December 21

The shortest day of the year: the sun rises at 8.04am and sets at 3.54pm. Druids celebrate the Winter Solstice at Stonehenge. A tornado uproots trees and damages buildings in West and East Stour, Dorset. Shrewsbury is on Flood Alert.

Friday
December 22

A giant mince pie is served at the Banqueting House in Whitehall, London, to celebrate the launch of the Academy of Culinary Arts. It contains 50.8kg flour, 27.2kg fat, 4.5kg caster sugar, 36 eggs, 45.4kg mincemeat and 2.3kg icing sugar!

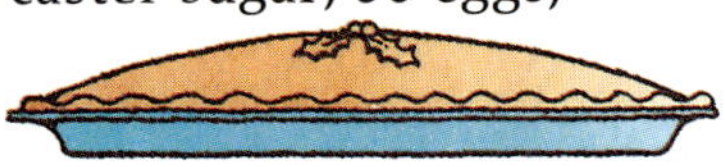

Saturday
December 23

23 yachts set off from Fremantle, Australia, to Auckland, New Zealand, on the third leg of the Whitbread Round the World Race.

Sunday
December 24

A huge 600sq km oil slick slithers towards the Atlantic coast of Morocco, after 168,000,000 litres of crude oil spills from the stricken Iranian tanker *Khark*.

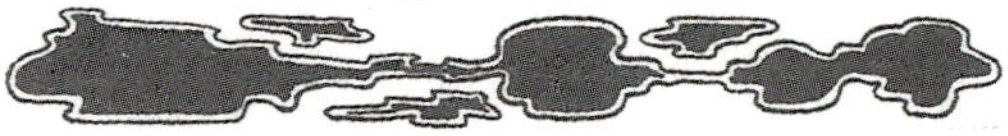

Monday
December 25

Christmas Day. Florida declares a State of Emergency as the southern states of the USA have their first white Christmas for 100yrs.

Tuesday
December 26

Boxing Day. 250yrs ago today, in 1739, the river Thames in London froze over and the nine-week London Frost Fair began.

Wednesday
December 27

A record 140 dogs have been rescued since Christmas Eve by the Battersea Dogs Home in London.

Thursday
December 28

South Yorkshire, West Yorkshire and the London Borough of Richmond come out as top recyclers in a Friends of the Earth recycling survey.

New Moon

Friday
December 29

The 2,000,000th car this year goes through Dover docks in Kent. Playwright Vaclav Havel becomes President of Czechoslovakia—the first non-communist to be elected for more than 40yrs.

Saturday
December 30

It's been the warmest year in Britain since records began in 1659: an average temperature of 10.7°C. There has been more sunshine than in any year since 1909 and less rain than in any year since 1976.

Sunday
December 31

An extra pip is added to the Greenwich time signal at midnight to bring our clocks exactly into line with solar time. It means that there are 86,401 seconds today—instead of the usual 86,400!